BLACK BEAUTY

TREASURY OF ILLUSTRATED CLASSICS™

BLACK BEAUTY

by
Anna Sewell

**Abridged, adapted,
and illustrated**
by
quadrum■

Modern Publishing
A Division of Kappa Books Publishers, LLC.

Cover art by Quadrum

Contents

CHAPTER 1

My Early Home

My earliest memory of home is that of a pleasant meadow with a pond of clear water in it. Water lilies grew in the deep end. Fir trees grew at the top of the meadow, and a brook lay at the bottom.

When I was little, I lived on my mother's milk since I could not eat grass. I ran beside her during the day and lay beside her during the night.

There were six other colts, older than myself. Some were as big as full-grown horses! I used to have lots of fun running everywhere with them. One day while I was playing, my

Black Beauty

mother called me. She said, "Listen carefully. The colts here are cart-horse colts and they've yet to learn manners. I hope you grow up to be gentle and good, never learn bad ways, work well, and trot well. Don't bite or kick while playing."

I have never forgotten my mother's advice. Our master was very fond of her. Her name was Duchess, but he often called her Pet. Our master was a good man. He spoke to us as he did to his children. He gave us good food and shelter. Whenever she saw him, she would go happily to him. He would pat her and ask, "Well, Pet, how is little Darkie?" Since I was dull black, he called me Darkie. I think we were his favorites.

Black Beauty

There was a plowboy, Dick, who sometimes came to our fields to pick blackberries. One day, he was throwing stones at us, not knowing the master was on the next farm. The master saw what Dick did, jumped over the fence, walked over to the boy, and gave him a box on the ear. "Bad boy! This isn't your first time, but it is definitely your last. Take this money and go home. Don't you ever come back!" So we never saw Dick anymore.

CHAPTER 2

The Hunt

I was not even two years old when the incident occurred in early spring. A light mist hung in the air. The colts and I were feeding at the lower part of the field. We heard dogs barking in the distance. The oldest of us pricked his ears. "Hounds!" he cried, and took off, followed by the rest of us, to the upper part of the field. My mother was standing there with an older horse.

"They found a hare," she said. "If they come this way, we'll be able to see the hunt."

Soon, the dogs were tearing through the wheat field next to ours. What noise they made! Following them were men on horseback, galloping as fast as they could. The old horse looked on eagerly while we colts felt the need to run with them. By the time they reached the lower fields, the dogs were running around with their noses to the ground.

"They've lost the scent," said the old horse. "Maybe the hare escaped."

Black Beauty

Before long, the dogs howled again and charged full speed toward our meadow and the steep banks that hung over the brook. "There's the hare," said my mother as the frightened animal scampered into the woods. The dogs followed and were upon her with their wild cries. We heard a loud shriek, and that was the end of her. The hunt was over.

I was so focused on what was happening there that I didn't see the sight at

Black Beauty

the brook. Two fine horses were down— one struggling in the stream, the other groaning on the bank. One of the riders was getting out of the water, covered with mud. The other lay very still on the bank. My mother told us he broke his neck.

"Serves him right," said one of the colts. I agreed, but my mother didn't.

Black Beauty

"You mustn't say that. I've seen and heard a lot during my time here. I've never understood why men are so fond of this sport. They get hurt often, spoil good horses, and tear up fields, all for a fox or a hare. But we are horses, and we don't know."

Many of the riders went to the fallen rider. My master, who saw the whole thing, was the first to raise him. His body lay limp. Everyone looked serious, even the dogs, for they sensed that something was wrong. I later heard that the poor rider was George Gordon, the squire's only son.

They rode off in different directions, some to the doctor and others to let the squire know what had happened. When someone checked on the horse lying on the bank moaning, he shook his head sadly. One of the horse's legs was broken. Someone ran to the master's house and came back with a gun. A loud bang, a sharp cry, and the black horse moved no more.

Black Beauty

My mother was quite troubled by this. She said she had known the horse for years and that his name was Rob Roy. He was a good horse, and there was no vice in him.

A few days later, we heard the church bell tolling for a long time and, looking over the gate we saw a long, strange black coach that was covered by a black cloth and was drawn by black horses. People dressed in black trailed this carriage taking young George for his burial. I don't know what they did with Rob Roy, but it was all for one little hare.

CHAPTER 3

My Breaking In

I was now beginning to grow handsome. My coat had grown fine and soft and was bright black. I had one white foot and a pretty star on my forehead. When I turned four, old Squire Gordon came to have a look at me and I trotted and galloped before him. He examined me thoroughly. He told my master, "When he has been broken in well, he will do fine." My master assured him that he would break me in himself. He lost no time and began the next day.

A breaking in means teaching a horse to wear a saddle and bridle, obey the master,

19

Black Beauty

and allow a man, woman, or child to ride him. The saddle wasn't so bad. My master put it on my back very gently while old Daniel held my head in a firm but gentle grip. He then fastened the girths under my body, all the while patting and talking to me. Then he fed me a few oats. He did this every day, until I started looking forward to the saddle and the oats. Finally, one morning, my master got on my back and rode me round the meadow. It felt a bit odd, but I felt proud to be carrying my master. He rode me every day, and soon I got accustomed to it.

Next was getting the iron shoes. That was unpleasant! My master took me to the smith's forge to see that the job was done without hurting me. The blacksmith took my foot in his hand and cut off a bit of the hoof. It didn't hurt me, so I patiently stood while he did the same with the other three legs. Then he took a piece of iron

the shape of my foot and clapped it on, and drove some nails through the shoe into my hoof so that the shoe was firmly on. My feet felt very stiff and heavy, but in time I got used to it.

Black Beauty

Then, my master got me used to the harness. There were more new things to wear. First, a stiff, heavy collar on my neck, and a bridle with great sidepieces against my eyes called blinkers. With the blinkers, I could only see straight, not side to side. Next, there was a small saddle with a nasty stiff strap that went right under my tail; that was the crupper. I hated the crupper; to have my long tail doubled up and poked through that strap was almost as bad as the bit. I never felt more like kicking, but of course I could not kick such a good master, and so in time I got used to everything and could do my work as well as my mother.

My master often drove me in double harness with my mother because she was steady and could teach me how to act better than a stranger could. She told me the better I behaved, the better I would be treated, and that it was wisest always to do my best to please my master. She also told me that

not everyone was as kind as he was. Most of all, she told me to keep a good reputation.

I was then sent to the neighboring farm for two weeks to experience the world beyond our meadow.

CHAPTER 4

Birtwick Park

Early in May, I was sold to Squire Gordon. My master came to me and said, "Good-bye, Darkie. Be a good horse and always do your best." And so I left my very first home.

Birtwick Park was a large estate with a large iron gate, the house, gardens, an orchard, and stables. There was room for many horses and carriages. The stable that I was in was quite roomy, with four good stalls, and a large swinging door that led to the yard, making the place more airy. The groom put me into this fine box. I was never

in a better box. The groom left after feeding me and talking nicely to me. While I ate my corn, I looked around.

In the stall next to mine was a small, fat, gray pony, with a thick mane and tail, a pretty head, and a pert little nose.

"How do you do?" I asked. "What's your name?"

"I'm Merrylegs. I'm quite handsome. I carry the ladies around and sometimes I take the mistress out on a low chair. Everyone likes me. Are you going to live right next to me?"

"Yes."

"Well, then," Merrylegs said, "I do hope you have a good temper. I don't like a neighbor that bites."

Just then, a horse's head looked over from the stall beyond. Its ears were laid back, and it looked quite ill-tempered. This was a tall, chestnut mare, with a long, handsome neck. She looked across to me and said, "So you've turned me out of my box. Strange thing for a young colt to turn a lady out of her own home!"

"I beg your pardon," I said. "I've turned no one out."

When she went out in the afternoon, Merrylegs told me that Ginger, the chestnut, had a bad habit of snapping and biting. She had the temper because of her former master's ill-treatment.

"I have noticed a change in her since she came here, though. It's because of the kindness with which John treats her."

CHAPTER 5

A Fair Start

The next morning, after grooming me nicely, the coachman, John Manly, took me out into the yard just as the squire came in to check on me.

"John, I wanted to try the new horse this morning, but I have other plans. You may as well take him around after breakfast and check his paces."

"I will, sir," said John. After breakfast, he came and fitted me with a bridle. He was very particular with the straps, seeing to it that my head passed through comfortably. Then he brought out a saddle that fitted nicely. He

rode
m   e
slowly at first,
then with a trot,
then with a canter, until
finally, with a light touch of his
whip, we were galloping.

"Ho, ho! My boy," he said as he pulled me up, "you would like to follow the hounds, I think."

We returned to see the squire walking with Mrs. Gordon. They stopped, and John jumped off.

"Well, John, how is he?" asked the squire.

"He's first class, sir," replied John. "He's as fast as a deer and has a fine sprint, too! Only the slightest touch of the reins will guide him."

"That's good. I'll try him out."

The next day I was brought up for my master. I remembered my mother's advice and I tried to do exactly what he wanted me to do. I found he was a very good rider, and thoughtful of his horse, too. When he came home, the lady was at the hall door as he rode up.

"Well, my dear," she said, "how do you like him?"

"He is exactly what John said," he replied. "A pleasanter creature I never wish to mount. What shall we call him?"

"Do you like Ebony?" she said. "He is as black as ebony."

"No, not Ebony."

"Will you call him Blackbird, like your uncle's old horse?"

"No, he is far handsomer than old Blackbird ever was."

"Yes," she said, "he is really quite a beauty, and he has such a good-tempered, sweet face, and such a fine, intelligent eye—what do you say to calling him Black Beauty?"

"Black Beauty—why, yes, I think that is a very good name. If you like it, it shall be his name." And so it was.

When John went into the stables, he told James that the master and the mistress had chosen a good English name for me. James said, "If it wouldn't bring up the past, I'd have called him Rob Roy, for I've never seen two horses more alike."

"No surprise there," said John. "Did you know that Farmer Grey's old Duchess was Rob Roy's mother as well?"

That was how I came to learn that Rob

Roy, who was killed during the hunt, was my brother. No wonder my mother was so upset!

John seemed very proud of me; he groomed me religiously every day until my coat outshone those of the other horses. I grew very fond of him. He was gentle and kind; he knew just how to make horses feel safe and happy. James Howard, the stable boy, was just as gentle and pleasant in his way, so I thought myself lucky.

A few days later, I had to go out with Ginger in the carriage. I wondered how we would get along, but surprisingly, she behaved quite well. John never had to use his whip on either one of us. I found it easy to trot beside her. After going out with her two or three times, we became quite friendly and sociable.

Merrylegs and I became great friends, too. He was such a cheerful, plucky, good-natured fellow, who was everyone's favorite. Our master had two other horses that stood

in another stable. One was Justice, a roan
cob, used for riding or for the luggage cart;
the other was an old brown hunter named
Sir Oliver.

CHAPTER 6

Freedom

Although I was happy in my new place, I longed for my freedom. For three years of my life I had all the liberty I could wish for; but now, week after week, month after month, and no doubt year after year, I would have to stand up in a stable night and day, except when I was wanted.

Straps here and straps there, a bit in my mouth, and blinkers over my eyes. It was uncomfortable for me, but this is the life of horses. For a young horse full of strength and spirit, who is used to a large

field or plain where he can fling up his head and toss up his tail and gallop away at full speed, it was difficult to stay in one place.

Sometimes, when I had less exercise than usual, I felt so full of life that when

John took me out of the stable, I could hardly control myself; but he was always good and patient.

"Steady, steady, my boy," he would say. "Wait a bit, and you will soon have your taste of speed."

Then, as soon as we were out of the village, he would give me a few miles at a spanking trot, and bring me back as fresh as before, only clear of the fidgets, as he called them. John had his own way of making me understand by the tone of his voice or the touch of the rein. If he was very serious and quite determined, I always knew it by his voice, and that had more power with me than anything else, for I was very fond of him.

We would have free time on Sundays. It was a great treat to us to be turned out into the home paddock or the old orchard. The grass was so cool and soft to our feet, the air so sweet, and the freedom to do as

we liked was so pleasant—to gallop, to lie down and roll over on our backs, or to nibble sweet grass. Then it was a very good time for talking as we stood together under the shade of the large chestnut tree.

CHAPTER 7

Ginger's Story

One day, Ginger and I had a long talk in which I told her about my upbringing and about my breaking in.

"Well," she said, "had I your turn off, I might've been better tempered. Now I don't think I can be anymore."

"Why not?" I asked.

"It was all so different for me," she said. "Nobody was kind to me, no one cared for me. As soon as I was weaned, I was taken away from my mother. The man who looked after us never said a kind word and, though

he never mistreated us, he didn't
do anything beyond feeding us. He
never spoke to us. There were a few
boys who would throw stones at us. I
was never hit, but one colt was; he got a
scar for life.

"When it came to my breaking in, it was
a nightmare. Several men came to catch me.
They cornered me. One held my forelock,
and another held my nose so hard, I couldn't
breathe; another took my jaw and wrenched
it open; then one dragged me by the halter,
and another kept whipping me. I gave them
plenty of trouble and was finally punished

by being locked up in the stall. It was utterly dreadful having your freedom taken away from you.

"My master's son was a strong, tall, bold man; they called him Samson, and he used to boast that he had never found a horse that could throw him. There was no gentleness in him, as there was in his father, but only hardness—a hard voice, a hard eye, a hard hand. I would be severely punished if I didn't do as he told me to.

"One day he had worked me hard in every way he could, and when I lay down I was tired, and miserable, and angry; it all seemed so hard. I had scarcely had an hour's rest when he came again for me with

Black Beauty

a saddle and bridle and a new kind of bit that was very painful. I reared up suddenly, which angered him, and he began to flog me. I couldn't take it, and I began to kick, and plunge, and rear as I had never done before, and we had a regular fight. At last after a terrible struggle I threw him off backward. I heard him fall heavily, and without looking behind me, I galloped off to the other end of the field.

"Soon, the old master came and with his kind voice he took away all my fears. He slowly led me to the stables, where Samson stood waiting. I laid back my ears and snapped at him. 'Stand back,' said the old man. 'You've not learned the trade yet. A bad-tempered man can never make a good-tempered horse.'

"He took me to the stall and cared for me with his own hands. He cleaned my wounds gently, all the while talking softly to me. He came to see me as often as possible. When I was fully healed, they called another breaker called Job. He was more thoughtful, and I soon learned what he wanted."

The next time Ginger and I were alone, she told me about her new home.

"After my breaking in, a chestnut horse and I were sold to a stylish gentleman who took us to London. I had been driven with a check-rein by the dealer, and I hated it worse than anything else; but the fashion called for it. We were often driven about in the park and other fashionable places. You've never heard of a check-rein? Let me tell you, it's dreadful.

"Imagine tossing your head high and holding it in place for hours, not being able to move it, having your neck go sore. I had two bits instead of one. Mine was sharp; it hurt my tongue and jaw, the blood from my mouth would color the froth. It was the worst when we had to stand by for hours waiting for our mistress at some grand party or entertainment, and if I fretted or stamped with impatience, the whip was laid on. It was enough to drive one mad.

"The master only wanted to look fashionable. He didn't know much about horses. With all the physical pain, I became more restless and irritable. I couldn't help it! I began snapping at anyone who came to harness me. I broke a lot of harnesses.

"I was soon taken to Tattersall's to be sold. The same dealer saw me and said he knew of a place that would suit me well. He said it was a pity that a fine horse like me should go to waste; and so I came here, not long before you did. But I'd already made up my mind about men being my natural enemies. It is very different here, but who knows how long it will last?"

"Well," I said, "it would be a real shame if you bit James or John."

"Not while they're good to me. I did

bite James once. John only told him to try me with kindness. Since then, James has treated me well. I've never snapped at him, and I never will."

I felt sorry for Ginger, and for all that she had been through. But I did see, in the weeks that followed, a considerable change come over her. She was more cheerful and gentle. One day James said, "I do believe the mare is getting fond of me!"

Our master noticed the change, too. One day he got down from his carriage and stroked her neck. "Well, my pretty," he crooned, "we shall make a cure of you."

CHAPTER 8

A Talk in the Orchard

When Mr. Bloomfield, the vicar, came visiting with his children, it was a lot of work for Merrylegs. They loved riding him and did so for hours.

One afternoon, James brought him back with the halter. "There, you rogue, behave yourself or we'll get in trouble," James said to him.

"What did you do?" I asked him.

"Oh, I've only been giving those young people a lesson," he replied. "They didn't know when to stop or when I'd had enough. So I just pitched them back, that's all."

"What?" I exclaimed. "You threw the children off? I thought you knew better than that. Did you throw Miss Jessie and Miss Flora off?"

Merrylegs looked a bit offended and replied, "Of course not! When it comes to the young ladies, I'm very careful. It's just that when the boys decided to play, they figured I'm a machine, never becoming tired, never running out. They didn't realize that I get tired, too. So I just rose on my hind legs and slipped one boy after another off my back. That's all I did! They aren't bad boys. I really do like them. It's just that I had to make them understand, and this was the only way."

"If I had been in your place," said Ginger, "I'd have given them each a good kick to teach them a lesson."

"Of that, my dear, I've no doubt!" said Merrylegs. "But no offense, I'm not such a fool. I don't want to anger the master or James. Plus, when those children are with me, they are my responsibility. If I took to kicking, where do you think I'd be? I'd be sold off in a jiffy! God knows under whose mercy I'd be. I could end up with a cruel master. No, I hope I shall never come to that."

One afternoon, all of us were grazing and talking under shady trees in an orchard. I stood next to Sir Oliver, an old and striking horse. I had often wondered how it was that Sir Oliver had such a very short tail; it really was only six or seven inches long, with a tassel of hair hanging from it. So I asked him one day how he had lost his tail.

"It was no accident!" he snorted. "It

was a cruel and shameful, cold-blooded act!
When I was young, I was taken to a place
where these cruel things were done. I was
tied up so that I could not stir, and then they
came and cut off my long and beautiful tail,
through the flesh and through the bone!"

"How dreadful!" I told him.

"Dreadful indeed! It wasn't just painful

physically; it was the indignity of having my best ornament taken from me. How could I ever brush the flies off my sides and hind legs anymore? You wouldn't know what it's like to lose a tail. Thank God they don't do it anymore."

"Why did they do it?" asked Ginger.

"For fashion—if you know what that means!" said the old horse with a stamp of his foot.

"I suppose it is fashion that makes them strap our heads up with those horrid bits with which I was tortured in London," said Ginger.

"But of course!" said Sir Oliver. "According to me, fashion is one of the wickedest things in the world. It is so painful. Why don't they cut their own children's ears into points to make them look sharp, or cut the end of their noses to make them look plucky? One would be just as sensible as the other. What rights have they to torment and disfigure God's creatures?"

Sir Oliver, though gentle, was a fiery old fellow, and what he said was all so new to me, and so dreadful, that I found a bitter feeling toward men rise up in my mind that I'd never had before. Ginger flung up her head and, with flashing eyes and distended nostrils, declared that men were both brutes and blockheads.

"Who talks about blockheads?" said Merrylegs, who just came up from the old apple tree, where he had been rubbing himself against the low branch. "I believe that is a bad word."

"Bad words were made for bad things," said Ginger, and she told him what Sir Oliver had said.

"It is all true," said Merrylegs sadly. "You know that the master, John, and James are always good to us, and talking against men in such a place as this doesn't seem fair or grateful; and you know there are good masters and good grooms beside ours, though of course ours are the best. So let us cheer up and have a run to the other end of the orchard. I believe the wind has blown down some apples and we might as well eat them."

Merrylegs could not be resisted, so we broke off our long conversation and raised our spirits by munching on some very sweet apples that lay scattered on the grass.

CHAPTER 9

Plain Speaking

I felt really proud and happy about living in a place like Birtwick. Our master and mistress were loved and respected by all who knew them.

The master and Farmer Grey worked together. If ever the mistress saw a heavily laden horse, she'd walk up to the owner and sweetly convince him that the way he was treating the horse was wrong. I wish all women were like her. Our master was also quite severe with those who mistreated horses.

Black Beauty

Once, while riding me home, he saw Sawyer whipping his horse for entering our lane instead of going straight. My master immediately demanded, "Isn't that horse made of flesh and blood?"

"Flesh, blood, and temper, sir," said Sawyer. "I don't like him going according to his own will. He wasn't supposed to take this turn. He came here on his own."

"You brought that pony here several times. The only reason he came here is because he remembers coming here. It shows his intelligence and memory. It gives me shame to witness this animal being treated this way by you."

Master rode me home slowly, and I could tell by his voice how the incident had grieved him. Another day, when we were out, we met Captain Langley, a friend of our master's; he was driving a splendid pair of grays in a kind of break. After a little conversation, the captain said, "What do you think of my new team, Mr. Douglas? You know you are the judge of horses in these parts, and I should like your opinion."

The master backed me a little, so as to get a good view of them. "They are an uncommonly handsome pair," he said, "and if they are as good as they look, I am sure you need not wish for anything better. But I see you still choke your horses, lessening

their power."

"What do you mean," said the captain, "the check-reins? Well, the fact is, I like to see my horses hold their heads up."

"As do I, and any other man," the master said, "but I don't like to see them held up. It takes all the shine out of them. You fret and worry their tempers, and decrease their power. You will not let them throw their weight against their work, and so they strain with their joints and muscles, and of course it wears them out faster. Besides, you know as well as I that if a horse makes a false step, he has much less chance of recovering himself if his head and neck are fastened back."

"I believe you are right," said the captain, and so they parted.

CHAPTER 10

A Stormy Day

One autumn day, my master had to go quite far on business. I was put into the dogcart, and John went with his master. I always liked to go in the dogcart. It was so light, and the high wheels ran along so pleasantly. There had been a great deal of rain, and now the wind was very high and blew the dry leaves across the road in a shower. We went along merrily till we came to the toll bar and the low wooden bridge. The man at the gate said the river was rising fast, and he feared it would be a bad night.

Many of the meadows were under water, and in one low part of the road, the water was halfway up to my knees. Master drove gently, so it was no matter.

We got to town, but my master's business had taken so long that we didn't leave until late afternoon. The winds grew stronger.

"I wish we were out of these woods,"

said my master.

"Oh, yes," agreed John, "it would be horrible to have one of these branches fall on us."

The words were scarcely out of his mouth when there was a groan, a crack, and a splitting sound. Crashing down among the other trees came an oak, torn up by the roots, and it fell right across the road just before us. I went still and I trembled a bit. John jumped out and came to me in a minute.

"That was close," said my master. "What do we do now?"

John replied that we would have to go back to the bridge, as there was no other way.

So back we went, and by the time we got to the bridge, it was nearly dark. Water had covered the middle part of it because of the floods. The moment my foot touched the bridge, I knew something was wrong. I didn't

Black Beauty

want to go forward and I stood in my place.

"Go on, Beauty," crooned my master. He gave me a light touch, but I didn't stir. He gave me a sharp whip, but I didn't move. John jumped out and came to me.

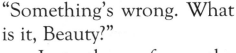

"Something's wrong. What is it, Beauty?"

Just then, from the opposite side, the man at the tollgate shouted at us, waving his torch like a madman. "Hoy! Stop there! Don't come farther!" he cried.

"What's wrong?" asked the master.

"The bridge is broken in the middle! Part of it got carried away. Had you tried crossing it, you would've been carried away by the current!"

"You saved us, Beauty!" John told me. He took the bridle and gently turned me around to the right-hand road by the riverside. The sun had set some time ago; the wind seemed to have lulled after the furious blast that tore up the tree. It grew darker and darker, stiller and stiller. I trotted quietly along, the wheels hardly making a sound on the soft road.

At last we came to the park gates and found the gardener looking for us. He told us that the mistress was quite worried about us being out in the storm. We saw a light at the hall door and at the upper windows, and as we came up, the mistress ran out, saying, "Are you really safe, my dear? Oh! I have been so anxious, imagining all sorts of things. Have you had an accident?"

"No, my dear. But had it not been for your Beauty, we'd have all been carried away with the water." I heard no more, as they went into the house, and John took me to the stable. Oh, what a good supper he gave me that night, and such a thick bed of straw! And I was glad of it, for I was tired.

CHAPTER 11

The Devil's Trademark

One day, John and I were returning after doing some work for the master when we saw a young boy trying to jump a pony over a gate. The pony wasn't making the jump. The boy got off, gave him a hard thrashing, and knocked him about the head; then he got up again and tried to make his pony leap the gate, kicking him all the time shamefully, but still the pony refused.

When we were nearly at the spot, the pony put down his head, threw up his heels, and sent the boy neatly over into a broad

hedge row. Then, with the rein dangling
from his head the pony set off home at a
full gallop. John laughed out loud. "Served
him right," he said.

"Ow!" cried the boy as he struggled among
the thorns. "Come and help me out. Please!"
cried the boy, quite entangled in a thornbush.
"Please help me!"

"You are where you deserve to be," said John. "Maybe the pricks will tell you not to make a pony jump over a gate that is too high for him." Saying this, we left.

"You know, Beauty," mumbled John, "I think we'd better go to Farmer Bushby and tell him what his son is up to."

"Have you seen my boy?" asked Mr. Bushby as we came up. "He went out an hour ago on my black pony, and the creature has just come back without a rider."

"I have, sir. It pains me to tell you that I just saw your son beating and kicking the pony mercilessly for not jumping over a gate too high for him. The horse didn't fight back, but in the end he pitched the boy into a hedge of thorns. The boy asked for my help, but, forgive me, I didn't do so. I love horses and I didn't like what he did to that pony one bit."

"Bill needs a lesson about this, and I must see that he gets it. This is not the first time that he has mistreated the pony, and I shall stop it. Good evening!"

So we went on, John chuckling all the way home. Then he told James about it, who laughed and said, "Serves him right. I knew him in school. He took great airs on himself because he was a farmer's son. He used to swagger about and bully other boys."

CHAPTER 12

James Howard

Early in December, after my daily exercise, John led me to my box. James was coming in from the corn chamber with some oats, when the master came into the stable. He looked rather serious, and held an open letter in his hand. "Good morning, John," said the master. "I want to know if you have any complaint about James."

"Complaint, sir? No, sir. He is a good lad, hardworking, and gentle with the horses."

The master called out to him, "James, put down that bag of oats and come here. I'm happy to find that John has the same

69

Black Beauty

opinion about you as I do. It's not easy to get a good opinion about someone from John! I have a letter from my brother-in-law, Sir Clifford Williams, of Clifford Hall. He wants me to find him a trustworthy young groom, about twenty or twenty-one, who knows his business. Sir Clifford is a good master, and if you could get the position, it would be a good start for you. Though I don't want to part with you, and if you left us, I know John would lose his right hand."

"That I should, sir," said John. "But he is as steady as a man, strong and well grown, and though he has not had much experience in driving, he has a light, firm hand and a quick eye, and he is very careful. Any horse will be lucky to have him look after it."

"Your word means a lot, John," said the master. "James, think it over, talk to your mother, and then let me know what you wish."

A few days later, it was settled that James was to go to Clifford Hall in a month's time. Till then, he was to practice driving as much as he could. Ginger and I were harnessed to the carriage, and James drove us. At first, John rode with him on the box, telling him

this and that, and after that, James drove
alone.

CHAPTER 13

The Fire

My master and mistress decided to pay a visit to friends who lived forty-six miles away. We went thirty-two miles on the first day. Even though there were some steep hills, we weren't worried, as James drove carefully. We stopped once or twice on the road, and just as the sun was going down, we reached the town where we were to spend the night. We stopped at the principal hotel, which was in the marketplace. It was a very large one. We drove under an archway into a long yard, at the farther end of which were the stables and coach houses. Two hostlers came to take us out. The head hostler, Dick Towler, was a pleasant, active little man, with a crooked leg and a yellow striped waistcoat.

The other hostler finished cleaning Ginger and brought us our corn. James left the stables with the old man and later came back again to see us one last time before he left, locking the doors behind him.

Later that night, I woke up feeling uncomfortable. The air felt thick and hot. I heard Ginger coughing and saw the other horses becoming restless. It was too dark to see, but I knew the stable was filled with smoke. I could barely breathe.

The trapdoor was open. I heard some crackling and snapping up in the loft, and I knew it wasn't good. The other horses also guessed that something wasn't right. I saw red light flickering. Just then, from outside, someone yelled, "Fire!" and the

Black Beauty

old hostler rushed inside. He started getting the horses out.

James came to me with his voice quiet and cheery: "Come, my Beauty, let us get out of this smoke." He took off his scarf and tied it over my eyes. He then led me outside. Once in the yard, he pulled the scarf off and shouted, "Someone take this horse while I get the other one!"

Black Beauty

Black Beauty

A tall man held me. As James ran inside I let out a shrill whinny. Ginger later told me that she got the courage to come out only because she heard the whinny and knew I was safe outside. I kept my eyes fixed at the door, hoping James and Ginger got out safe. I heard my master behind me: "James Howard! Where are you?"

Just then, something crashed in the stable. I was relieved to see Ginger and James running out. She coughed a lot, and James couldn't breathe or see clearly. My master went to him and asked him if he was hurt. James shook his head.

"We have to get out of here," the master said. As we hurried from that place, Ginger and I heard a terrible sound that made us feel horrible; we heard the frightened and piercing shrieks and neighs of the horses that were still inside, burning to death. We were quite upset but at the same time we were glad to make it out alive.

Black Beauty

The next morning, the master came to see how we were and to speak to James. He then went to hear more about the fire.

Apparently at first no one could guess how the fire had been caused, but at last a man said he had seen Dick Towler go into the stable with a pipe in his mouth, and when he came out, the pipe was missing. Then the under hostler said he had asked Dick to go up the ladder to put down some hay, but told him to lay down his pipe first. Dick denied taking the pipe with him, but no one believed him.

James said the roof and floor had all fallen in, and that only the black walls were standing; the two poor horses that could not be got out were buried under the burnt rafters and tiles.

CHAPTER 14

Good-bye, James

The remainder of our journey went well. Soon, we reached our destination. The stable we went to was very nice; the coachman made us very comfortable and thought a great deal of James because of what he had heard.

"There's something very good about you," he told James. "The horses know how to trust you. It's difficult to get them out of the stable during fire or floods. But you managed!"

We stayed there for two or three days,

Black Beauty

then returned home. John was quite happy to see us, as much as we were happy to be home. Before he and James left us for the night, James said, "I wonder who is coming in my place."

"Little Joe Green at the lodge," said John. He also said that though the boy was only fourteen, he was bright and was willing to help out.

The next day Joe came to the stables to learn all he could before James left. He learned to sweep the stable and to bring in the straw and hay; he began to clean the harness, and helped to wash the carriage. He couldn't groom Ginger or me, as he was very short. He was a nice little bright fellow, and

always came whistling to his work.

Merrylegs was quite upset about being groomed by a boy who knew nothing; but toward the end of the second week he told me that he thought the boy would do well.

At last the day came when James had to leave us; he looked quite downhearted that morning.

"Cheer up, James," said John. "You'll make friends there. And if you get on well, as I am sure you will, it will be a fine thing for your mother, and she will be proud enough that you got into such a good place as that."

Everyone was sorry to lose James. Merrylegs didn't eat for many days. So on several mornings when John exercised me, he took Merrylegs along with a leading rein. And trotting and galloping by my side, the little fellow's spirits were lifted, and he was soon all right.

CHAPTER 15

Going for the Doctor

One night after James left, I was sleeping in the stable when I was awakened by the stable bells ringing loudly. John hurried to me and woke me up. "Come on, Beauty, we have somewhere to go to—and fast!"

Before I could think, he had me saddled and ready. As we rushed out, the butler stopped him at the door.

"Now, John," he said, "ride fast for your mistress's life; there is not a moment to lose. Give this note to Dr. White. Give your horse a rest at the inn, and be back as

Black Beauty

soon as you can."

The gardener, who lived at the lodge,
heard the bell ring and was ready with the
gate open, and away we went through the
park and through the village. A nice long
stretch of road lay beside the river. John

told me to do what I did best, and I did. I covered two miles so fast, I didn't think my old grandfather, who had won the race at Newmarket, could have beaten me. John praised me when we reached the bridge. He would've preferred if I had slowed down, but I was too energized to do so. We reached the village when everyone there was asleep. The church tower had struck three.

We went to Dr. White's door, where John rang the doorbell twice and then knocked like thunder. The doctor poked his head, with a nightcap on it, out the window and asked, "What do you want?"

"Mrs. Gordon is very ill, sir. Master wants you to go at once. He thinks she will die if you cannot get there. Here is a note."

"Wait," he said. "I will come." He shut the window, and was soon at the door.

"The worst of it," he said, "is that my horse has been out all day and is quite done up. And my son has just been sent

Black Beauty

for, so he has taken the other horse. Can I use yours?"

"He has come at a gallop nearly all the way, sir, and I was going to give him a rest here; but I think my master would not be against it, if you think fit, sir."

"All right," he said. "I will soon be ready."

John stood by me and stroked my neck; I was very hot. The doctor came out with his riding whip.

"You need not take that, sir," said John. "Black Beauty will go till he drops. Take care of him, sir, if you can. I should not like any harm to come to him."

"No, no, John," said the doctor, "I hope not." And in a minute, we had left John far behind.

The doctor was a heavier man than John, and not so good a rider; however, I did my very best. The man at the tollgate had it open. When we came to the hill, the doctor drew me up. "Now my good fellow," he said, "take some breaths." I was glad he did, for I was nearly spent, but that breathing helped me on, and soon we were in the park. Joe was at the lodge gate; my master was at the Hall door, for he had heard us coming. He spoke not a word; the doctor went into the house with him, and Joe led me to the stable.

I was glad to get home; my legs shook under me, and I could only stand and pant. I had not a dry hair on my body, sweat ran down my legs, and I steamed all over. Poor Joe rubbed my legs and my chest, but he did not put my warm cloth on me; he thought I was so hot, I should not like it. He gave me a bucketful of water to drink. It was cold and very good, and I drank it all; then he gave me some hay and some corn and, thinking he had done right, went away.

Soon I began to shake and tremble, and turned deadly cold; my legs ached, my loins ached, and my chest ached, and I felt sore all over. Oh! How I wished for John, but he had eight miles to walk, so I lay down in my straw and tried to go to sleep.

After a long while I heard John at the door; I gave a low moan, for I was in great pain. He was at my side in a moment. I could not tell him how I felt, but he seemed to know it all; he covered me up with two or three warm cloths, and then ran to the house for some hot water. He seemed to be very much put out. I heard him say to himself over and over again, "Stupid boy! No cloth put on, and nothing given to eat." But Joe was a good boy, after all.

I was very ill; a strong inflammation had attacked my lungs. It was painful to breathe. John nursed me night and day; he would get up two or three times in the night to come to me. My master also came to see me. "My poor Beauty," he said one day, "my good horse, you saved your mistress's life." I was very glad to hear that, for it seems the doctor had said if we had been a little longer, it would have been too late. John told my master he never saw a horse go so fast in his life. It seemed as if the horse knew what the matter was. Of course I did.

I knew that John and I must go at the top of our speed, and that it was for the sake of the mistress.

CHAPTER 16

Joe Green

I didn't know how long I was ill. Mr. Bond, the horse doctor, came to see me every day. Ginger and Merrylegs had been moved elsewhere, so I had nothing but quiet around me.

One day, while John was giving me a draught to make me sleep more easily, Thomas Green entered the stables and walked over to John.

"Please talk to Joe. He's feeling horrible about what happened. He blames himself completely and has stopped taking his meals. He is sure he is at fault, though he

Black Beauty

truly thought he was doing the right thing. He says no one will ever speak to him again if Beauty dies; it hurts to hear him say that. He really is a good boy."

John told him, "Don't be so hard on me, Tom. I know the boy meant well when he did what he did. But that horse is very dear to me, and to think he might lose his life in such a way is more than I can bear. But if you think I've been hard on the boy, I will try to give him a good word tomorrow—that is, I mean if Beauty is better."

"Well, John, thank you. I know you do not wish to be too hard, and I am glad you see it was only ignorance."

John's voice almost startled me as he answered: "Only ignorance! How can you talk about only ignorance? Don't you know that it is the worst thing in the world, next to wickedness?"

I heard no more of this conversation, for the medicine did well and sent me to sleep, and in the morning I felt much better; but I often thought of John's words when I came to know more of the world. Under John's instructions, Joe turned out very well. He was a fast and attentive learner.

One day, John was out with Justice in the luggage cart, and the master wanted a note to be taken immediately to a gentleman's house, about three miles away. He sent his orders for Joe to saddle me and take it, advising him to ride steadily.

The note was delivered, and we were quietly returning when we came to the brickfield. Here we saw a cart heavily laden with bricks; the wheels had stuck fast in the stiff mud of some deep ruts, and the carter was shouting and flogging the two horses unmercifully. Joe pulled up. It was a sad sight. There were the two horses straining and struggling with all their might to drag the cart out, but they could not move it; the man, fiercely pulling at the head of the frontmost horse, swore and lashed at them most brutally.

"Don't flog them like that!" said Joe. "The wheels are too stuck for them to move ahead! I'll help you make the cart light so they can move."

"You mind your own business, boy, and I'll do mine," growled the man. The man towered over Joe and was a bit drunk. He continued to lash at the horses. Joe turned my head, and the next moment we were going at a round gallop toward the house of the master brick maker. I cannot say if John would have approved of our pace, but Joe and I were of one mind, and so angry that we could not have gone slower.

The house stood close by the roadside. Joe knocked at the door and shouted, "Hello! Is Mr. Clay at home?" The door was opened, and Mr. Clay himself came out.

"Hello, young man! You seem in

a hurry. Any orders from the squire this morning?"

"No, Mr. Clay, but there's a fellow in your brickyard flogging two horses to death. I told him to stop, and he wouldn't. I said I'd help him lighten the cart, and he wouldn't. So I have come to tell you. Pray, sir, go." Joe's voice shook with excitement.

"Thank ye, my lad," said the man, running in for his hat. Then, after pausing for a moment, he said "Will you give evidence of what you saw if I should bring the fellow up before a magistrate?"

"That I will," said Joe, "and gladly, too." The man was gone, and we were on our way home at a smart trot.

"Why, what's the matter with you, Joe? You look angry all over," said John as the boy flung himself from the saddle.

"I *am* angry all over, I can tell you," said the boy, and then in hurried, excited words he told all that had happened. Joe was usually such a quiet, gentle little fellow that it was wonderful to see him so roused.

"Right, Joe! You did right, my boy, whether the fellow gets a summons or not. Many folks would have ridden by and said it was not their business to interfere. Now I say that with cruelty and oppression it is everybody's business to interfere when they see it; you did right, my boy."

Joe was quite calm by this time, and proud that John approved of him. He cleaned out my feet and rubbed me down with a firmer hand than usual.

They were just going home to dinner when the footman came down to the stable to say that Joe was wanted directly in his master's private room; there was a man brought up for ill-using horses, and Joe's evidence was wanted.

The boy flushed up to his forehead, and his eyes sparkled.

"They shall have it," he said.

"Straighten yourself out," said John. Joe gave a pull at his necktie and a twitch at his jacket, and was off in a moment. Since our master was one of the county magistrates, cases were often brought to him to settle or to say what should be done.

In the stable we heard no more for some time as it was the men's dinner hour, but when Joe came next into the stable, I saw he was in high spirits. He gave me a good-natured slap and said, "We won't see such things done, will we, old fellow?"

We heard afterward that he had given his evidence so clearly, and the horses were in such an exhausted state, bearing marks of such brutal usage, that the carter was committed to stand trial, and might possibly be sentenced to two or three months in prison.

Black Beauty

It was wonderful what a change had come over Joe. John laughed and said he had grown an inch taller in that week, and I believe he had. He was just as kind and gentle as before, but there was more purpose and determination in all that he did—as if he had jumped at once from a boy into a man.

CHAPTER 17

The Parting

It had been three happy years since I had lived here. But all good things must come to an end. Our mistress fell ill from time to time. We heard that she must leave and go to a warm country for two or three years for her health to improve. Our master began arranging for them to leave England. Everybody was sorry to hear the news; it was all we talked about in the stables. John went about his work silently, and Joe rarely whistled.

Miss Jessie and Miss Flora were the first ones to leave with their governess.

They came to bid us good-bye. They hugged poor Merrylegs like he was an old friend, and indeed he was. We heard about our arrangements. Master had sold Ginger and me to his old friend, the Earl of W——, as he thought we should have a good place there. Merrylegs was given to the vicar, who wanted a pony for Mrs. Bloomfield, but it was on the condition that he should never be sold. Joe was engaged to take care of

him and to help in the house, so I thought that Merrylegs was well off. John had the offer of several good places, but he said he should wait a little and look around.

The evening before they left, the master came into the stable to give some directions and to give his horses the last pat. He seemed very low-spirited; I knew that by his voice. I believe we horses can tell more by the voice than many men can.

"Have you decided what to do, John?" he said. "I find you have not accepted any of those offers."

"No, sir. I have made up my mind that if I could get a situation with some first-rate colt breaker and horse trainer, it would be the right thing for me. Many young animals are frightened and spoiled by wrong treatment, which need not be if the right man took them in hand. I always get on well with horses, and if I could help some of them to a fair start, I should feel as if I were doing some good. What do you think of it, sir?"

"I think you are well suited for it. You have a way with horses. It is what you're best at. If you need any help, write to me. I'll speak to my agent in London and put in a good word for you."

Master gave John the name and address, and then he thanked him for his long and faithful service. Master gave John his hand, but he did not speak, and they both left the stable.

The next day, the master and the mistress had to leave. The footmen and the luggage had gone earlier. It was only the master, the mistress, and the maid. Ginger and I brought the carriage to the door for the last time. The servants brought out cushions and rugs and many other things, and when all were arranged, the master came down the steps carrying the mistress in his arms. He placed her carefully in the carriage while the house servants stood around crying.

"Good-bye, again," he said. "We shall not forget any of you." Then he got in. "Drive on, John," he said.

When we arrived at the railway station, the mistress went to the waiting room. I heard her say good-bye to John in her sweet

voice. John couldn't speak. Poor Joe was nearly in tears. Very soon the train came puffing up to the station; then, after two or three minutes, the doors were slammed. The guard whistled, and then the train glided away, leaving behind it only clouds of white smoke and some very heavy hearts. When it was quite out of sight, John came back.

CHAPTER 18

Earlshall

The next morning, Joe came to say good-bye to us, while Merrylegs neighed at us from outside. John then led Ginger and me fifteen miles away to Earlshall Park, where the Earl of W—— lived. It was a grand house with a fine stable. John asked for Mr. York, our new coachman. He was a fine-looking, middle-aged man, and his voice was firm. He was very friendly and polite to John, and after giving us a quick look, he called a groom to take us to our boxes and invited John to take some refreshment.

Black Beauty

We were taken to a light, airy stable, and placed in boxes next to each other, where we were rubbed down and fed. Soon, John and Mr. York returned.

"Now, Mr. Manly," said Mr. York, "we all know that each horse has its own personality and its own way of being treated. Is there anything in particular you'd like to tell me about these two?"

"Well, sir, I don't believe there is a finer pair of horses than this one. They have different natures. The black one has the most perfect temper. He quite loves to please you and do as you ask. But the chestnut is a bit snappish; I suspect this is because of her bad treatment when she was a foal. If you treat her well, she'll be willing to do anything for you."

"Of course," said York, "I quite understand. I'll remember what you have said about the mare."

They were going out of the stable when John stopped and said, "I must tell you we have never used the check-rein with either of them; the black horse never had one on, and the dealer said it was the gag-bit that spoiled the other's temper."

"Well, if they come here they must wear the check-rein. I prefer a loose rein myself, and his lordship is always very reasonable about horses; but my lady, she insists on it."

"That's bad," said John. "Now I must leave, or I shall miss my train."

He came around to pat and speak to us for the last time; his voice sounded very sad.

I held my face close to him; that was all I could do to say good-bye. And then he was gone, and I have never seen him since.

The next day Lord W—— came to look at us. York then told him what John had said about us.

"Well," he said, "you must keep an eye on the mare, and use the check-rein sparingly. I feel they will do very well with a little humoring at first. I'll mention it to your lady."

In the afternoon we were harnessed and put in the carriage, and led around to the front of the house. It was all very grand, and three or four times as large as the old house at Birtwick, but not half as pleasant. Two footmen were standing ready, dressed in drab livery, with scarlet breeches and white stockings. Presently we heard the rustling sound of silk as my lady came down the flight of stone steps. She stepped around to look at us; she was a tall, proud-looking woman and did not seem pleased about something, but she said nothing and got into the carriage.

This was the first time of wearing a check-rein. I felt anxious about Ginger, but she seemed to be quiet and content. York came around to our heads and shortened the rein himself—one hole, I think; every little bit makes a difference, be it for better or worse, and that day we had a steep hill to go up. Then I began to understand what I had heard about the check-rein. I had to pull the carriage with my head up now, and that took all the spirit out of me, and the strain came on my back and legs. When we came in, Ginger said, "Now you see what it is like; it just gets worse. I won't take it if I don't like it. I won't!"

Day by day, hole by hole, our bearing reins were shortened, and instead of looking forward with pleasure to having my harness put on, I began to dread it. Ginger, too, seemed restless, though she said very little. For several days there was no more shortening, and I thought the worst was over. But the worst was yet to come.

CHAPTER 19

A Strike for Liberty

One day, my lady came down later than usual, and the silk rustled more than ever. "Drive to the Duchess of B——'s," she said; and then, after a pause: "Are you never going to get those horses' heads up, York? Raise them at once and let us have no more of this humoring and nonsense."

York came to me first, while the groom stood at Ginger's head. He drew my head back and fixed the rein so tight that it was almost intolerable; then he went to Ginger, who was impatiently jerking her head up and down against the bit. She knew what was coming, and the moment York took the rein off the terret in order to shorten it, she took her opportunity and reared up so suddenly that York had his nose hit and hat knocked off; the groom was nearly thrown off his legs. At once they both flew to her

head; but she was a match for them, and went on plunging, rearing, and kicking in a desperate manner. At last she kicked right over the carriage pole and fell down, after giving me a severe blow on my near quarter.

The groom soon set me free from Ginger and the carriage, and led me to my box and ran back to York.

Before long, however, Ginger was led in by two grooms, a good deal bruised. York came with her and gave his orders, and then came to look at me. In a moment he let down my head.

"Confound these check-reins!" he said to himself. "I knew we would have some mischief soon. Master will be sorely vexed. It's all because of the check-reins. I knew they would bring trouble. If only the mistress weren't so stubborn about it!"

Lord W—— was much put out when he learned what had happened; he blamed

York for giving in to his mistress, to which York replied that in the future, he would much prefer to receive his orders only from the master. I thought York might have stood up better for his horses, but perhaps I am no judge.

Ginger was never put into the carriage again, but when she was healed from her bruises, one of the master's younger sons said he should like to have her; he was sure she would make a good hunter. As for me, I was obliged still to go in the carriage, and had a fresh partner called Max; he had always been used to the tight rein. I asked him how it was he bore it.

"Well," he said, "I bear it because I must. But it is shortening my life, and it will shorten yours, too, if you have to stick to it."

"Do you think," I said, "that our masters know how bad the check-rein is for us?"

"I can't say," he replied, "but the dealers and the horse doctors know it very well.

The horses soon wear out, or get diseased, and they come for another pair."

For the next four months, I suffered in those reins. I even began foaming at the mouth, something I never did before. There was a lot of pressure on my windpipe.

Black Beauty

In my old home I always knew that
John and my master were my friends; but
here, although in many ways I was well
treated, I had no friend. Even though York
knew the reins were troubling me quite a
bit, he did nothing to relieve me of the
pains.

CHAPTER 20

Lady Anne
on a Runaway Horse

Early in spring, Lord W—— and his family went to London, and took York with them. His daughters Lady Harriet and Lady Anne stayed back. Lady Harriet was an invalid and never went out in the carriage, and Lady Anne preferred riding on horseback with her brother and cousins. Ginger, some other horses, and I were left at home, and the head groom was in charge. Lady Anne was very good on horseback. She was gentle and

beautiful. She chose me for her horse and called me Black Auster. I enjoyed my rides with her; sometimes we rode with Ginger and Lizzie, another horse. This Lizzie was a bright bay mare, almost Thoroughbred, a favorite with the gentlemen, on account of her fine action and lively spirit; but Ginger, who knew more of her than I did, told me she was rather nervous.

A gentleman named Colonel Blantyre stayed at the Hall; he always rode Lizzie, and praised her so much that one day Lady Anne ordered the sidesaddle to be put on her, and the other saddle on me. The gentleman seemed very uneasy.

"Do not mount her," he said. "She is a charming creature, but she is too nervous for a lady. I assure you, she is not safe."

"Dear cousin," she said, "don't worry about me. I've been riding ever since I was a baby! I've hunted with hounds, and I know you don't like it. I want to try Lizzie and see what you men like about her so much. So help me up!"

Without saying another word, he put her carefully on Lizzie, and then mounted me. We went to Dr. Ashley's. The village was about a mile off, and the doctor's house was the last in it. There was a short drive up to the house between tall evergreens.

Blantyre alighted at the gate and was going to open it for Lady Anne, but she said, "I will wait for you here."

While we waited, some cart horses and several young colts came trotting out in a very disorderly manner, while a boy behind was cracking a great whip. The colts were wild, and one of them bolted across the road and bumped Lizzie's hind legs. She gave a violent kick and dashed off into a headlong gallop. It was so sudden that Lady Anne was nearly unseated, but she soon recovered herself.

I gave a loud, shrill neigh for help. Blantyre came running to the gate and saw them moving faster and farther away. He mounted me and charged forward. Several times we saw them, and then lost them.

Black Beauty

However, it was clear that the roughness of the ground had slowed Lizzie down, and there seemed a chance that we might overtake her.

With a light hand and a practiced eye, Blantyre guided me over the ground in such a masterly manner that my pace was hardly slowed down, and we were decidedly gaining on them. About halfway across the open rough land, there was a freshly dug ditch, and the loose earth from the digging was piled up on the other side.

Lizzie took the leap, stumbled on the loose mud, and fell. Blantyre groaned, but gave me a steady rein. I gathered my courage and, with one determined leap, cleared the ditch.

My mistress lay with her face to the ground. When Blantyre turned her, her face was white and her eyes were closed. "Oh, God! Anne!" He unbuttoned her habit, loosened her collar, felt her hands and wrists, then started up and looked wildly around him for help.

Some distance away, there were two men cutting turf, who, seeing Lizzie running wild without a rider, had left their work to catch her.

Blantyre's cry soon brought them to the spot. The foremost man seemed much troubled at the sight, and asked what he could do.

"Can you ride?"

"Sir, I'm not much of a horseman. But I'd risk my neck for Lady Anne."

"Mount this horse, my friend, and go to the doctor. Tell him to come immediately. Then go to the Hall. Get Lady Anne a carriage and her maid."

The man scrambled onto my back and we took off, with him holding on to me for dear life. After we alerted the doctor and rode back to the Hall, I was taken to my box, where I was unsaddled and cooled.

Ginger was saddled in my stead and off she went at full speed. It took a long time before she returned. She then told me what had happened. She told me that Lady Anne wasn't dead. The doctor had poured something into her mouth.

Two days after the accident, Blantyre paid me a visit; he patted me and praised me very much. I understood that my young mistress, Lady Anne was now out of danger and would soon be able to ride again. This was good news to me.

CHAPTER 21

Reuben Smith

Let me tell you a bit about Reuben Smith, who was in charge of the stables when York left for London. He was a man who knew his business well. He was a first-class driver, handsome, and intelligent. And he had pleasant manners. His only problem was that he loved to drink. Though he didn't drink regularly, when he did, he'd become a terror to his wife and a nuisance to others. But he was so useful that York himself kept the matter from the earl. Smith had promised faithfully that he would never

drink. He had kept his promise so well that York thought he might be safely trusted when he was away.

Colonel Blantyre was returning to his regiment. It was arranged that Smith should drive him to the town. At the station Blantyre put some money into Smith's hand and bid him good-bye, saying, "Take care of your young mistress, Reuben, and don't let anyone but the mistress ride Black Auster."

We left the carriage at the maker's, and Smith rode me to the White Lion. He ordered the hostler to feed me well and have me ready for him at four o'clock. A nail in one of my front shoes had started to come out; the hostler noticed it at just about four o'clock. Smith came out an hour later and said he would not leave till six, as he had met with some old friends. The hostler then told him of the nail, and asked if he should have the shoe fixed.

"No," said Smith.

I found it odd that he didn't check the shoes, for it was one of the things he was particular about. He left and didn't return until nine, when he called for me. It was with a loud, rough voice. He seemed in a very bad temper, and abused the hostler. Almost before he was out of the town,

he began to gallop, frequently giving me a sharp cut with his whip, though I was going at full speed. The moon had not yet risen, and it was very dark. The roads were stony, and going over them at this pace, my shoe became looser and then it came off.

Had Mr. Smith been in his senses, he'd have understood that something was wrong in my movement. But he was too drunk to notice. Fresh stones with sharp edges had just been laid and I was forced to go fast on this road, with one shoe gone. My shoeless foot suffered dreadfully; the hoof was broken and split, and the inside was terribly cut by the sharpness of the stones.

I couldn't take the pain anymore. I collapsed, and Smith was flung off my back with great force. He was lying a few yards from me and was silent for a bit. Then I heard a loud moan. I would've moaned,

too, for I had severe pain in my foot and knees. But I didn't, for horses bear pain in silence. I stood up with much effort and listened for a sound, but all I got was silence.

It must have been nearly midnight when I heard the sound of a horse's feet. As the noises came closer, I could make out Ginger's steps. I neighed loudly and was

glad to hear a neigh from her. Men came over the stones slowly and stopped over the figure that lay on the ground.

A man bent over him and examined him. "His body's cold," he said. "Reuben's dead."

They raised his lifeless body, his hair soaked in blood. They laid him down again and came to me. They saw the cuts on my knees.

"The horse went down with him, too! His foot's gone bad. Look, his hoof is cut up into pieces. Reuben was drunk, for sure. If he wasn't, he wouldn't have ridden the horse the way he did."

I shall never forget that night's walk; it was more than three miles. Robert led me on very slowly, and I limped and hobbled as well as I could, with great pain. I am sure he was sorry for me, for he often patted and encouraged me, talking to me in a pleasant voice.

At last I reached my own box, and had some corn; and after Robert had wrapped up my knees in wet cloths, he tied up my foot in a bran poultice, to draw out the heat and cleanse it before the horse doctor saw it in the morning. I managed to get myself down on the straw, and slept in spite of the pain.

The next day, after the doctor had examined my wounds, he said he hoped the joint was not injured. I believe they did their best to make a good cure, but it was a long and painful one.

As Smith's death was so sudden, there was an investigation about it. But all the evidence and statements given by witnesses about Reuben being drunk and my shoe being loose helped me get clear of any blame.

CHAPTER 22

Ruined and
Going Downhill

As soon as my knees healed, I was turned
out into a small meadow for a month
or two. No other animal was allowed there.
Although I enjoyed my solitude and the
sweet grass, part of me longed for company.
I missed Ginger, for we had become quite
good friends.

One morning the gate was opened and
who should come in but dear old Ginger.
The man slipped off her halter and left her

Black Beauty

there. With a joyful whinny, I trotted up to
her; we were both glad to meet, but I soon
found that it was not for our pleasure that
she was brought to be with me. She had
been ruined by hard riding because of Lord
George, and was now dismissed to see what
some rest would do.

Ginger told me, "Lord George
is young and will take no advice; he
hunts whenever he can get the chance,
quite careless of his horse. Though the
groom told him I was unfit to ride in a

steeplechase, he was determined to ride me. He was too heavy for me and strained my back.

"And so," she said, "here we are, ruined in the prime of our youth and strength, you by a drunkard, and I by a fool; it is very sad." We both felt in ourselves that we were not what we had been. However, that did not spoil the pleasure we had in each other's company, and so we passed our time till the family returned from town.

One day we saw the earl come into the meadow, and York was with him. They came up to us and examined us carefully. The earl seemed very annoyed.

"My old friend thought his horses would have a good home with me, and now they are ruined," he said. "The mare shall have a twelve-month run, but the black one must be sold. With those scarred knees, I can't have him in my stables anymore."

"No, my lord, of course not," said York.

"But he might get a place where appearance is not of much consequence, and still be well treated. I know a man in Bath, the master of some livery stables, who often wants a good horse at a low figure. I know he looks well after his horses."

After this, they left us.

"They'll soon take you away," said Ginger, "and I shall lose the only friend I have, and most likely we shall never see each other again!"

I was bought by the master of the livery stables. I had to go by train, which was new to me, and required a good deal of courage the first time. When I reached the end of my journey I found myself in a tolerably comfortable stable, and well attended to. I was well fed and well cleaned, and, on the whole, I think our master took as much care of us as he could.

In my new place, I experienced all

kinds of bad and inexperienced driving. I was what they called a "job horse." I was given out to all those who wished to hire me. There were many styles in which I was driven. Some drivers were often careless altogether, and attended to anything but their horses. I went out in the phaeton one day with one of them; he had a lady and two children behind. He flipped the reins about as we started, and of course gave me several unnecessary cuts with the whip, though I was moving quickly

already. The road was being made and there were many loose stones lying about. I ended up getting a stone in one of my forefeet. The stone was so sharp, it could make it easy for me to stumble and fall.

Whether that man was blind or ignorant, I didn't know, but he drove me for half a mile with that stone in my foot. By that time I was going so lame with the pain that at last he saw it, and called out, "Why, they have sent us out with a lame horse! What a shame!"

He then chucked the reins and flipped about with the whip, saying, "Now, then, it's no use playing the old soldier with me; there's the journey to go, and it's no use turning lame and lazy."

Just at this time, a farmer rode up on a brown cob. He waved his hat to stop us, dismounted, and came to me. He lifted my foot and removed the stone with a little difficulty. I walked ahead, glad to have the stone gone, but still bearing the pain. I had many people like him ride or drive me.

A few months later, I was taken out by a man who really knew to ride—I was so happy! The man liked me so much, he urged my master to sell me to a friend who wanted a gentle horse like me. And so, I was sold, that summer, to Mr. Barry.

CHAPTER 23

A Thief

My new master was an unmarried man, living in Bath. His doctor advised him to take horse exercise, and for this purpose he bought me. He got a stable a short distance from his lodgings, and engaged a man named Filcher as groom. My master knew very little about horses, but he treated me well, and I should have had a good and easy place but for circumstances of which he was ignorant. He ordered the best hay with plenty of oats, crushed beans, and bran, with vetches, or rye grass. I thought I

Black Beauty

was quite well off.

For a few days, all went well. I found that my groom understood his business. He kept the stable clean and airy. He groomed me thoroughly and was never anything but gentle.

But then, after a while, the quality of my food started to change for the worse. In two or three weeks, this began to tell upon my strength and spirits. Of course, I couldn't complain to anyone.

After two months of inferior feed, I wondered if my master knew this was happening. One afternoon, he rode out into the country to see his friend, a gentleman farmer who had a very keen eye for horses. After he had welcomed my master, this gentleman cast his eye over me, saying, "Well, Barry, it seems to me that your horse doesn't look as well as he did when you first had him; hasn't he been eating well?"

"Yes, I believe so," said my master,

Black Beauty

"but he is not nearly so lively as he was. My groom tells me that horses are always dull and weak in the autumn, and that I must expect it."

The other shook his head slowly and began to feel me all over.

"I can't say who eats your corn, my dear fellow, but it surely isn't the horse. Have you ridden very fast?"

"No, very gently."

"Then just put your hand here," said he, passing his hand over my neck and shoulder. "He is as warm and damp as a horse just come up from grass. I advise you to look into your stable a little more. There are mean scoundrels, wicked enough to rob a dumb beast of his food. Give this horse a right good feed of bruised oats, and don't stint him."

Dumb beasts! Yes, we are. But if I could have spoken, I would have told my master where his oats went. They went off with his groom and his boy, that's where!

Five or six mornings after this, the stable door was pushed open and a policeman walked in, holding the child tight by the arm; another policeman followed, and locked the door on the inside, saying, "So those oats you're carrying are for your father's rabbits, hey? Show me the place where he keeps their food."

The boy led the way to the corn bin. Here, the policeman saw that it was empty, and there was another full bag of feed, like the one the boy had. The policeman realized that the boy had stolen my food.

Filcher was cleaning my feet at the time, but the police accosted him, and though he blustered a good deal, they walked him off to the "lockup," and his boy with him. I heard afterward that the boy was not held to be guilty, but the man was sentenced to prison for two months.

CHAPTER 24

My New Master

My master hired a handsome new groom called Alfred Smirk. At first, he seemed like a good man and took proper care of me. But things began to change. He started neglecting me. The man was interested in nothing but his good looks. He stopped exercising me and didn't clean the litter in my stall. As a result, I got a bad infection on my hooves from standing in the dirty stall all day. When Mr. Barry found out, he was so upset about being cheated by two grooms that he decided he no longer wanted to own a horse. I soon found myself for sale at a horse fair. I was shown with two or three good horses, and many people came to see us. I was thoroughly examined by all, both gently and roughly. One kind man, who I hoped would buy me, offered a good price, but was denied. A hard-looking man made his offer. I thanked God when he was refused, too. Two or three more made their offers. Just then, the hard-looking man, as well as the kind one, came back and started a bidding war. The kind man finally won the bidding, and I was his. He fed me a few oats, spoke softly to me while I ate, and then took me home.

After a long ride, he pulled up near a small house and whistled. The door opened, and out ran a woman followed by a girl and a boy who happily greeted their father. They immediately ran to me and patted me and spoke to me in soft voices. I felt happy to be here! Jeremiah Baker—

Black Beauty

or Jerry, as most called him— was my new master. His wife, Polly, was attractive, with smooth, dark hair and a smiling mouth. The boy, Harry, was about twelve, a good lad, and the girl was Dorothy, or Dolly, age eight. They loved one another very much, and I was glad to be a part of this family.

Jerry drove a cab in the city. I was to be paired up with a horse called Captain. The next morning, Polly and Dolly came to the stables to make friends with me. They talked to me, fed me juicy apples, and cooed over my damaged knees. It was decided that they would call me Jack, after their old horse.

That afternoon, I was put into the cab for the first time. Jerry was careful to see that the collar and bridle were comfortable. Thankfully, there was no check-rein. In the city, Jerry drove proudly and showed me off to his colleagues. Many thought there must be something wrong with me, as I was too fine-looking for a cab horse. But Jerry

Black Beauty

smiled with pride.

The first week was a little difficult, as I wasn't used to the city and the noise. But I got to trust Jerry and soon got used to it all. In no time, Jerry and I got along very well. We understood each other! Captain and I even had a day off on Sundays. We became friendly; we would use our Sundays to talk and enjoy each other's company. I learned a lot about Captain; he was broken in as an army horse, but after seeing so much bloodshed and death, he didn't want to be in the army anymore. In time, our friendship grew even more. I loved my new home, and started feeling like my old self again.

CHAPTER 25

Jeremiah Baker

I never knew a better master than Jerry. He was kind and stood up for what he believed in. He was quite good- natured. He liked making songs and singing to himself. One he was very fond of was this:

"Come, father and mother,
And sister and brother,
Come, all of you turn to
And help one another."

The entire family would pitch in one hundred percent in whatever work they did. One thing he hated was seeing people whip horses to go faster. He could not bear any careless loitering and wasting of time; nothing was so near to making him angry as people who were late and wanted a cab horse to be driven hard in order to make up for their idleness.

One day, two wild-looking men came out of a tavern and hailed Jerry: "Here, cabbie! Look sharp! We are rather late. Put on the steam, will you? And take us to the Victoria Station in time for the one o'clock train. You shall have a shilling extra."

"I will take you at the regular pace, gentlemen. Shillings don't pay for putting on the steam like that."

Jerry convinced them that he'd take them at a safe pace and get them there in time with no extra charge. The men agreed. Although Jerry was determinedly set against hard driving to please careless people, he always went a good fair pace, and was not against putting on the steam, for a good reason.

Now, driving through a crowded city can be difficult. But if you have a good driver and horse, there was nothing to it! Jerry and I were used to the crowded streets, so we went through easily. In no time, we

reached the station with five minutes to spare! The men were very pleased and relieved and thanked Jerry.

"Thank God, we made it! And thank you, my friend, and your horse." They offered Jerry more money, but he refused, taking only what was charged. He helped the men with their bags and saw them disappear into the crowd. We felt really good helping people this way.

CHAPTER 26

Poor Ginger

One day, while our cab and many others were waiting outside a park, a shabby old cab pulled up next to ours. The horse was a tired chestnut with a bad coat and with hardly any flesh on her. Her forelegs were very shaky. I was eating hay when a gust of wind blew some of it toward her. She stretched her long, thin neck and ate the hay, and then she looked around for more. There was hardly any life in her eyes. She looked so familiar, though! Before I could say anything, she looked at me and asked in a tired voice,

Black Beauty

"Black Beauty, is that you?"

It was Ginger! God, how she had changed! Her beautiful arched and glossy neck had sunken through, her legs were out of shape, and her face bore signs of pain and torment. She even had trouble breathing because of her coughing. Somehow, she was able to tell me what had happened since I had left.

After the twelve-month run at Earlshall, she had been sold again. For a little while things had gone well, but after a longer gallop, the old strain had returned. After a short rest, she had been sold again. She was sold many times, and each time to a more demeaning rank.

"Finally," she said, "I was bought by a man who kept cabs and horses and rented them out. When he found out my weakness, he said that I wasn't worth the money he had paid. I was to be put on a small cab and just be used up. That is what they are doing. They whip me and work me without a thought. I don't even have a day off," she ended sadly.

"But why didn't you stand up for yourself like you used to?" I asked her.

"What is the use of it if you'll be overpowered? Men are cruel and have no feelings. I wish I was dead so I would not have to bear this anymore."

I felt so upset to hear her say that. I put my nose up to hers, yet there was nothing I could do to comfort her. She looked at me for a moment, then said, "You look well off, Beauty. I'm so glad." She paused, and then added, "You're the only friend I've ever had."

Just then, her driver came back and, with a tug at her mouth, drove off, leaving me feeling utterly sad. A few days later, a cart carrying a dead horse passed our cab stand. I saw the dead horse, and my blood ran cold. What a horrible sight! The head was hanging out of the cart, and blood dripped

from the mouth. It was a chestnut horse with a long, thin neck. I think it was Ginger. I hoped it was she, for then her suffering would be over. Oh! Had men been more kind, they'd have shot us before allowing us to suffer like this.

CHAPTER 27

Jerry's New Year

Christmas and New Year's are when people spend most of their time with family and friends celebrating and not worrying about having any work to do. But it's not like that for Jerry and me. In fact, this is the time we work the most! There are so many people who go around the cities to parties, and we drive them around till late in the night. Sometimes the driver and his horse have to wait in the rain or snow while his passengers are inside dancing and celebrating with

family and friends.

Jerry had a terrible cough during Christmas week, during which we worked a great deal. But however late we were, Polly would always greet us at the door with a lantern in her hand. She often looked worried about Jerry's health. On New Year's Eve, we dropped off two gentlemen to a house in one of the city squares by nine o' clock. They told us they'd return by eleven.

Black Beauty

They added that they could be a few minutes late, but we should wait still. We waited till eleven, we even waited till midnight, but the men still didn't come back. The wind was strong, cold, and hard. Jerry pulled one of my blankets around my neck. He was coughing badly and there was no shelter around. A little after one, the men came out, got into the cab, and told us where to go. My legs were so numb, I thought I'd fall. The men didn't even apologize for making us wait.

We finally got home. Jerry couldn't talk, and his cough was worse than ever. As tired as he was, he fed me and gave me a good rubdown. The next morning, Harry came to clean and feed us. I could sense from his movements that something was wrong. I soon heard Polly telling the children that their father was very ill. For three days we thought he wouldn't recover. Finally, Polly gave the news that Jerry was out of danger.

Black Beauty

The doctor told him not to drive a cab again. Soon after, Jerry received a letter from an old widow telling him to come as her coachman. There was a good school as well for the children. It was decided that they would move to the country as soon as Jerry was better. The sad news was that I had to be sold again. I loved my master and my new home, but there was no other option. When that day came, I couldn't even see Jerry, as he was too weak to get up from bed. Polly and the children came to see me off. Polly stroked me and told me she wished I could've come with them. She kissed my neck softly, and I was led away.

CHAPTER 28

Jakes and the Lady

I was sold to a corn dealer and baker whom Jerry knew. He was sure I would have a good life there. Jerry would've been right except my new owner was not around to supervise his workers. The foreman went about ordering everyone to work faster and faster. Many times, my cart would be loaded with more goods than I could comfortably pull. Jakes was my driver, and he always told the foreman that the load I carried was too much. But the foreman always ignored him as he was only a worker.

I had to wear a check-rein this time as well. I wore it for four horrid months, pulling those heavy loads. I felt my strength failing me again. One day, I had to carry the goods uphill. I tried so hard, but I couldn't do it. I stopped. Jakes became angry and started shouting at me.

"Get moving, lazy fellow, or I'll whip you!" he said.

He whipped me, over and over again. Just as I thought I couldn't take it anymore, I heard a woman crying out, "Please don't

hit him like that! He's a good horse and I'm
sure he's trying his best. Take off the check-
rein and I know he'll do better."

"All right. Anything to please a woman,"
said Jakes with a laugh. After he loosened
my reins, I put my head down for a few
moments, then tossed it up and down to
get the stiffness off my neck.

"Poor fellow," crooned the lady.
"You must've had the check-rein on for
a long time!"

Black Beauty

I threw my weight against my collar and got the load up the hill. The lady came and patted my neck. How good it felt to be patted again after so long. She asked Jakes to remember that it is very difficult for a horse to pull a cart uphill with a check-rein and she hoped he wouldn't use it again. After she left, he considered her words, then decided to give me a loose rein. Even then, my workload was heavy. I grew more tired with each day. Eventually I wasn't able to do my share of work. So I was sold again to a large cab owner.

CHAPTER 29

Hard Times

My new master owned a fleet of cabs. He was a cruel-looking man with black eyes, a hooked nose, and a hard, harsh voice. His mouth was always in a snarl. His name was Nicholas Skinner. Until now, I'd never known the miseries of a common cab-horse.

Skinner owned shabby cabs, driven by second-rate drivers. He was hard on his men; and they in turn were hard on their horses. We were made to work long hours in the summer heat. Sometimes I had to drive a group of men out into the country on Sundays. I was forced to go up and down steep hills as fast as possible. After such rides, I felt so feverish and worn out that I could hardly eat. How I longed for the bran mash that Jerry used to give me.

My new driver was a hard man. He had a whip with something so sharp at the end, it would draw blood. He'd whip me under my belly at times and even whip my head. All these things made me feel that life was not worth living. I missed the soft caresses and the kind words Jerry and his family gave me. I was so miserable that I wished, like Ginger, I was dead so that I wouldn't have to suffer anymore. One day, my wish almost came true.

I'd done a good share of work that morning when we had to take a man to the station. After that man left, a family of four came and asked the driver if he'd take them to town. They had a lot of heavy luggage

Black Beauty

with them. While the father loaded the bags, the girl looked at me and said, "Papa, I'm sure this poor horse cannot take us and all our luggage so far into town. He looks so tired and weak. Do look at him."

"Not to worry, miss," said the driver. "He's stronger than he looks." To show them exactly that, he began to load the heaviest trunks onto the cab. In the end, the load was very heavy and I was tired and hungry. In spite of this cruelty, I did my best. I moved along well enough, until we came to a steep hill. My own exhaustion and the heavy load were far too much to bear, coupled with the lashes I kept getting on my back. Suddenly, I felt my knees buckle and I fell to the ground. I was so drained, I didn't have the strength to move. Pandemonium rose all around me. I heard angry voices and sounds of the luggage being unloaded. I even heard a sweet voice saying, "Oh, that poor horse! It's all our fault!"

I didn't open my eyes. I only gave short, gasping breaths. Someone came and loosened the strap of my bridle and undid my collar. Cold water was thrown over my head and some of it was put in my mouth. I was covered with a blanket, and I lay there on the cold street for a long time. I soon felt my strength coming back to me. A kind-voiced man was patting me gently and was encouraging me to get up. After a

couple of attempts, I staggered to my feet and was led to a stable nearby. I was put in a comfortable stall and was given warm food. That evening, I was well enough to be led back to my own stable. In the morning, Skinner came to look at me.

"He's done for. I'd have given him six months to rest completely, but I don't have time or money to nurse a sick horse. I'm going to sell him."

He gave me ten days of rest and good food, at the end of which I thought it was definitely better to live than die. I was then taken to a fair in London. I felt that any other place would be better than my present place, so I held my head high and hoped for the best.

CHAPTER 30

Farmer Thoroughgood and His Grandson Willie

A t this fair, I was put up for auction with old, broken-down horses. Poor farmers were trying to sell off their old horses for some money. The buyers and sellers didn't look much better off than those in the last fair. Poverty had hardened all of them, and I ached to hear a kind voice, a voice I could trust.

My gaze fell on a farmer with a small boy. The farmer had a kind look about

him. I pricked my ears and looked at him. I heard him telling the boy that I was a horse who had seen better days.

"He must've been something when he was young, Willie," he said.

He stuck out his hand and patted my neck, and I stuck out my nose. The boy leaned forward and stroked my face. "Look, Grandpa! He can understand kindness. Poor fellow! Can we buy him and make him feel good again? Please, Grandpa!" the boy pleaded. He even insisted that I was not old, just worn out and in need of some rest.

The farmer laughed and felt my legs, which were so swollen and strained. He looked at my mouth and then at his grandson's begging face. He sighed and nodded his approval. The boy jumped for joy. I would've, too, if my legs were not so bad. The farmer's name was Mr. Thoroughgood. His grandson, Willie, was assigned to take care of me. I was given hay and oats all the time, and I was made to

run in the meadow during the day. Willie gave me many carrots and stood by me for hours petting me.

My health and condition improved steadily. My legs soon became fit again. I pulled Willie and his grandfather in a fine carriage all the way to town. The farmer was very proud and pleased. He and Willie decided to find me a good home where I would be loved and valued.

CHAPTER 31

My Last Home

One day, during summer, the groom cleaned and brushed me with such care that I knew something different was happening today. Willie looked excited and nervous as he got into the carriage with his grandfather.

"If the women like him," said the old man, "they will be happy, and so will he."

We traveled for a mile or two till we reached a small house with a large lawn and lots of trees. Three elderly women came to meet us. They seemed quite lively and were excited to see me. One of them, Miss

Ellen, liked me immediately. The tall, pale lady said that she would always be nervous riding behind a horse that had once been down, as it could happen again. If it did, she would never get over the fright.

"You see, ladies," said Mr. Thoroughgood, "many first-rate horses have had their knees broken through the carelessness of their drivers, without any fault of their own, and from what I see of this horse, I should say that is his case. But of course I do not wish to influence you. If you are so inclined, you can have him on trial, and then your coachman will see what he thinks of him."

"You have always been such a good adviser to us about our horses," said the stately lady, "that your recommendation goes a long way with me, and if my sister Lavinia sees no objection, we will accept your offer of a trial, with thanks."

It was then arranged that I should be sent for the next day.

In the morning, a smart-looking

young man came for me. At first he looked
pleased; but when he saw my knees, he said
in a disappointed voice, "I didn't think, sir,
that you would have recommended such a
blemished horse to my ladies."

"Handsome is that handsome does,"
said my master. "You are only taking him
on trial, and I am sure you will do fairly by
him, young man. If he is not as safe as any

horse you ever drove, send him back."

I was led to my new home, placed in a comfortable stable, fed, and left to myself. The next day, when the groom was cleaning my face, he said, "That is just like the star that Black Beauty had; he is much the same height, too. I wonder where he is now."

A little later, he began to look me over carefully, talking to himself.

"White star on the forehead, white foot, that little patch of white on the back." He stopped and looked at my face, and into my eyes.

"I don't believe it! Black Beauty? Is that you? Oh, my God! It is you! Oh, I do hope you remember who I am. Joe Green! Remember little Joe Green who almost killed you by accident that cold night?"

I could not say that I remembered him, for now he was a fine, grown-up young fellow, with black whiskers and a

man's voice, but I was sure he knew me, and that he was Joe Green, and I was very glad. I put my nose up to him and tried to say that we were friends. I never saw a man so pleased.

Once he calmed down, he said in a softer voice, "I wonder who that rascal is who broke your knees. You weren't so well off, were you? Don't you worry. I'll make sure nothing bad happens to you again. How I wish John Manly were here to see you!"

Joe ran back to the house after seeing that I was settled and told Miss Ellen that I was Squire Gordon's Black Beauty. She was thrilled and decided to write a letter to Mrs. Gordon, telling her that her favorite horse had come back. They decided to keep my name Black Beauty.

I've lived in this place for more than a year now. Joe is the best and kindest groom I've ever had.

Willie always speaks to me when he can, and treats me as his special friend. My ladies have promised that I shall never be sold, and so I have nothing to fear; and here my story ends. My troubles are all over, and I am at home; and often before I am quite awake, I dream I am still in the orchard at Birtwick, standing with my old friends under the apple trees.

About the Author

Anna Sewell was born in 1820 to a religious Quaker family in Great Yarmouth, England. She spent her childhood in London and its suburbs. Anna was very much influenced by her mother's religious and educational beliefs.

At the age of fourteen, Anna became an invalid for life due to an ankle injury. She could not stand without the help of crutches, nor could she walk. To move around, she preferred horse-drawn carriages. This increased her love and affection for animals, especially horses.

Black Beauty was written between 1871 and 1877. It is the only book she wrote. During this period her health was failing her. She was often so weak that she couldn't get out of bed, and even writing was a challenge. She died on April 25, 1878, just a few months after the book was published. She lived long enough to see her creation become a huge success.

The Adventures of Tom Sawyer
The Adventures of Pinocchio
Alice in Wonderland
Anne of Green Gables
Beauty and the Beast
Black Beauty
The Call of the Wild
A Christmas Carol
Frankenstein
Great Expectations
Journey to the Center of the Earth
The Jungle Book
King Arthur and the Knights of the Round Table
Little Women
Moby Dick
The Night Before Christmas and Other Holiday Tales
Oliver Twist
Peter Pan
The Prince and the Pauper
Pygmalion
The Secret Garden
The Time Machine
Treasure Island
White Fang
The Wind in the Willows
The Wizard of Oz